The Veiled Definition And The Door Of No Return

A Compilation of Letters and Notes

BARBARA F. COTTON, JD

Warrior Princess Nation, LLC

THE VEILED DEFINITION AND THE DOOR OF NO RETURN

Copyright © 2024 by Barbara Cotton

Contents

Dedication

This book is dedicated to the reader... May you have a profound experience of Ephesians 1:17-19 AMPC

And for Tamir, Elijah, Noah, Ayden, and Qualia.

And for my mother, who, to this day, I can remember lovingly saying, "Look it up" in answer to my many questions.

Forward

Attached is a sentence outline draft, which is submitted to you because of the urgency of the moment. Initially written in 2019-2020 and beyond, the present zeitgeist shift compels me to submit it to you in its draft form. Time and security are therefore of the essence...As a 74-year-old Christian from Oakland, CA, and in the attitude of a griot, this information ultimately belongs to *The People*.

Because the Harlem Renaissance was successfully relabeled by Carl Van Vechten's paradigm shift (lest history repeats itself or William Lloyd Garrison notwithstanding), I am compelled to very calmly arm the reader with the very best arguments and tools for deprogramming racist *strongholds* that God has given me. It is imperative (because of the polarities) that the contents be prayed over and pondered. Proverbs 1:6 King James & Amplified. The book "Nigger Heaven" is Carl Van Vechten's relabeling/reframing of the Harlem Renaissance phenomenon. Suffice it to say that this betrayal and outrage should not be dignified by being typed. Nevertheless, on the surface, it is a reference to the balcony of a 19th-century church. This writer takes exception to its use as a reference point for many reasons. However, its existence is germane to "The Veiled Definition and the Door of No Return" and is therefore referred to in this way. Consequently, polarities and layers abound.

W.E.B. Dubois and his concept of Double Consciousness is cited, as well as the likes of F. Scott Fitzgerald, the cousin of Francis Scott Key, the composer of the Star Spangled Banner (Colin Kaepernick's protest song) from opposite ends of the spectrum. Both symbolize Double Consciousness, but the enemy even went so far as to *create* an artificial intelligence corporate *person* (which enjoys perpetual existence) in answer to the 14th Amendment and Reconstruction. See Santa Clara V. Southern Pacific Railroad Co. 118 US 394 (1886). However, it is the Word of God that is alive! Hebrews 4:12 AMP.

You will be inspired by studying how definitions can be veiled and the consequences thereof, such as Revelation 22:18-19 AMP. See, The Negro Bible, by Joseph Lumpkin.

You will be galvanized by seeing the Statue of Justice as an enigma through the eyes of Joel Augustus Rogers, visionary, and galvanized by *classical* education and by Darwin, whose theories are much more harmful and dangerous (As an open secret!) than Critical Race Theory (CRT.)

That being said, let us paradigm shift CRT with emphasis on history to CRT with emphasis on history **plus** hermeneutics (interpretation), thereby incorporating such principles as Scripture into the picture.

Jesus Christ has paid the price of our passage into the heavenly realm where there is no segregation but *includes* many of our ancestors and is full of moral power and excellence of soul.

For the kingdom of God consists of and is based on not talk but power (moral power and excellence of soul). 1 Corinthians 4:20 AMPC

Dunamis (power) and eternal life (perpetual existence)

We will transition smoothly from self to the body of Christ in a *cultural revelation*, an awakening, Revelation 3:8, where great suffering is rewarded with great personal growth.

> *I know your [record of] works and what you are doing. See! I have set before you a door wide open which no one is able to shut; I know that you have but little power, and yet you have kept My Word and guarded My message and have not renounced or denied My name. Revelation 3:8 AMPC*

> *[But what of that?] For I consider that the sufferings of this present time (this present life) are not worth being compared with the glory that is about to be revealed to us and in us and for us and conferred on us! Romans 8:18 AMPC*

> *Which is His body, the fullness of Him Who fills all in all [for in that body lives the full measure of Him Who makes everything complete, and Who fills everything everywhere with Himself]. Ephesians 1:23 AMPC*

Please handle this writing with the utmost discretion, as the inference that black supermen and superwomen are developing may be found in this writing. Viz., The more suffering, the more personal growth. See John 16:33:

> *I have told you these things, so that in Me you may have [perfect] peace and confidence. In the world you have tribulation and trials and distress and frustration; but be of good cheer [take courage; be confident, certain, un-daunted]! For I have overcome the world. [I have deprived it of power to harm you and have conquered it for you.] AMPC*

"Overcome the world..." And despite Brittanica's, The Great Books of the Western "World," the formulaic structure of Scripture may be remembered and memorized with relative ease.

Remember the days of old; consider the years of many generations. Ask your father and he will show you, your elders, and they will tell you. Deuteronomy 32:7 AMPC

I remember the days of old; I meditate on all Your doings; I ponder the work of Your hands. Psalm 143:5 AMPC

Finally, perhaps herein is an incentive for reprobates and malfeasants to repent and DO GOOD. Proverbs 9:10, The fear of the Lord is the beginning of wisdom, and the knowledge of the Holy One is understanding; (unveiling...Revelation 1:1; and open door...Revelation 3:8.)

And now here is a cautionary hypothetical, "The Veiled Definition..."

Chapter 1

The Mars Analogy Hypothetical

Martians Land snatching 12.5 million White Americans from their homes and breeding men, women, and children for a **race** of sub-Martian slaves, separating families - Wiping out the memory of Earth by forcing the Martian language and forbidding reading and writing and using **slave breakers** to break the resistant men, women, and children.

Racialized policing has begun...judge, jury, and executioners.

Imagine:
12.5 million humans of **reproductive** age. What would that do to the advancement of Earth? Industry? Science? Medicine? Sociology? Religion?

An error compounded over 100s and 100s of years...

"Be patient," they are told...

A Veil (a forfeited ability to communicate, understand, and interpret) has been tightly interwoven into the fabric of the Martian persona and the American Earthlings - who are persona non grata.

The definition of forfeiture is the giving up of something as a "penalty" for wrongdoing.

Chapter 2

End of Hypothetical

The Interpretation Penalty or Veiled Christianity is here called "The Veiled Definition."

The Door of No Return: one of many in Africa through which Africans were pushed into slavery in America, is both an entrance and an exit.

Psalm 119:130 says:
"The entrance of your (God's) words give light; their unfolding gives understanding to the simple."

African slavery in North America ostensibly ended in 1863 with the Emancipation Proclamation. Yet systemic oppression and racism have persisted into the 21st century. In fact, it is an epidemic in America and has been since 1619 - over 400 years ago...

This paper will address two of the veiled surviving roots of the epidemic in 21st-century America.

Darwin's natural selection (commonly regarded as evolution theory) and social Darwinism (commonly regarded as survival of the fittest). It will address the fervent outcry and lack of direction, which is presently resulting in a kind of en masse post-traumatic stress disorder (PTSD) for not only blacks but also some whites as well. Moreover, it is this writer's contention that blacks, in particular, have been forced into a condition best characterized as "bipolar."

Quote from J.A. Rogers (1880-1966) Harlem Renaissance Bibliophile, Journalist, and Historian. From Superman to Man; "Justice, when the Negro is brought before her, discards her scales and takes a firmer grip on her sword."

This statement paints a vivid picture of the effects of PTSD on the African-American.

W.E.B. Dubois (1868-1963), Harlem Renaissance Sociologist, Philosopher, Journalist, and Co-Founder of the NAACP, referred to it as a concept that he called "2-ness" or double consciousness.

His "striving" and "of the coming of John" (2 Johns) chapters stand out as poignantly and graphically illustrative of these concepts. Dubois also makes mention of the concept of *the veil*. The veil prevents many white people from seeing black people as American - or even fully human.

Also taken from his 1903 anthology, The Souls of Black Folk, Dubois coined the phrase: "The problem of the 20th century is the problem of the color line." The term "color line" was coined by Frederick Douglass (1818-1895)

And, alas, here in the 21st century, African Americans are still grappling with the myth of being regarded as sub-human. (See Zallinger's March of Progress).

See 2 Corinthians 3:14-17; the veil is taken away upon REPENTANCE.

Our youth are indoctrinated early into 2-ness or double consciousness. In this context, bipolar disorder and PTSD are a result of racial polarization.

"The talk" and "the look" are concepts that black parents are forced to teach young people as a consequence of racism. And it is an exercise in futility to avoid it because if you are black and Christian in the secular world of social Darwinism, it is unavoidable, especially when the curse of Ham and survival of the fittest persist as pejorative codes which suggest that to be black or dark is to be inferior.

It is pejorative if you are black, but in the words of the likes of F. Scott Fitzgerald: "The test of a 1st rate intelligence is the ability to hold two opposed ideas in the mind at the same time and still retain the ability to function."
e.g. Law School Exams or Black History Recitations

Codes suggest the underlying intent of implied inferiority.
Curse: Genesis 9:24-27
Reversed: Galatians 3:13

Blacks as persona non grata: Unwelcomed or unacceptable is nothing new.

Beneath the Veil (Song of Solomon 1:5-7 KJV is online currently and overtly being changed from "I am black" to "I am dark or swarthy or tan," but the tents of Kedar were blue-black. New American Standard "Swarthy," New King James, "Dark/Tan," Good News Translation, "Dark/Tanned," NIV "Dark." Even Emerson said, "When it is dark enough, you can see the stars."

In fact, there are many Scriptures that extol darkness - not the kingdom of darkness, but darkness nonetheless.

They are:
Darkness as good

I will open my mouth in a parable (in instruction by numerous examples); I will utter dark sayings of old [that hide important truth] Psalm 78:2 AMPC

Even the darkness hides nothing from You, but the night shines as the day; the darkness and the light are both alike to You. Psalm 139:12 AMPC

He made darkness His secret hiding place; as His pavilion (His canopy) round about Him were dark waters and thick clouds of the skies. Psalm 18:11 AMPC

Then Solomon said, The Lord has said that He would dwell in the thick darkness; I have built You a house, [in which the dark Holy of Holies seems] a [fitting] abode for You, a place for You to dwell in forever. 2 Chronicles 6:1-2 AMPC

And I will give you the treasures of darkness and hidden riches of secret places, that you may know that it is I, the Lord, the God of Israel, Who calls you by your name. Isaiah 45:3 AMPC

Then Solomon said, The Lord said that He would dwell in the thick darkness.1 Kings 8:12 AMPC

"I have told you these things in figurative language (veiled language, proverbs); the hour is now coming when I will no longer speak to you in figures of speech, but I will tell you plainly about the Father. John 16:25 AMP

I will submit and consent to a parable or proverb; to the music of a lyre I will unfold my riddle (my problem). Psalm 49:4 AMPC

I am black, but comely, O ye daughters of Jerusalem, as the tents of Kedar, as the curtains of Solomon. Look not upon me, because I am black, because the sun hath looked upon me: my mother's children were angry with me; they made me the keeper of the vineyards; but mine own vineyard have I not kept. Tell me, O thou whom my soul loveth, where thou feedest, where thou makest thy flock to rest at noon: for why should I be as one that turneth aside by the flocks of thy companions? Song of Songs 1:5-7 KJV

To understand a proverb, and the interpretation; the words of the wise, and their dark sayings. Proverbs 1:6 KJV

Chapter 3

Being Down In The Dumps Is Brought About By Thought Police

Whether called a paradigm shift, Orwellian doublethink, or Social Darwinism, the "doldrums" are brought about by misinformation and omission of meanings beyond the surface (micro-aggression escalating to macro-aggression). The techniques of omission and misinformation can be fully ascertained by the fact that the secular world's omission of Scriptures *and* history leaves us with cognitive dissonance...or could Fitzgerald's 1st rate intelligence be produced?

For example, online, many black scholars from the period of the Harlem Renaissance, such as W.E.B. DuBois, Joel Augustus Rogers, and Carter G. Woodson, are listed as freethinkers (or atheists) in order to *discourage* black Christians from actually reading and studying their important work. Why, even Frederick Douglass is listed as a freethinker! These literary giants and dedicated public servants are segregated into "Black History Month" but are totally obfuscated as unbelievers!

The inability to acknowledge God's providence is perpetuated in schools, but Jesus is freely encouraged in prisons...!

Take, for example, the fact that God has been removed from public schools, but Darwin's natural selection theory is still taught in many schools, pop culture, TV, and online. (It is a far cry from the language of the Declaration of Independence.)

In 1859, Charles Darwin (1809-1882) in what is generally understood as the proponent of his *evolutionary theory* - to this day fails to state the full title of his treatise, which is:
    "The Origin of Species by Means of Natural Selection - or the Preservation of Favored Races in the Struggle for Life." (1859)

If there is still any doubt as to Darwin's meaning and intent, in 1871, he is quoted as saying in, The Descent of Man and Selection on Relation to Sex: "The civilized races of man will almost certainly exterminate and replace the savage races through the world." (Spencer)

A Struggle for Existence = Existential Crisis

The above-referred quotes are demonstrative of a *spirit* of struggle. Is it any wonder that there are so many frustrated and directionless people? And violence?

But the morbidity does not stop there. In 1860, Darwin devolved into saying: "I care more about Drosera than all the species in the world." (And not the metamorphosis of the butterfly chrysalis, as one might imagine!)

Drosera is a carnivorous plant. Darwin's degenerative theories are a devolution rather than an evolution, a spirit realm *door of no return*. The dynamic at work is capture/entrapment/consumption of the substance of the prey. The same systemic dynamic in the form of racism is at work in America and is a root of racism in America.

Historic and socioeconomic consumption of black substance is apparent in the SPP school-to-prison pipeline and in the absence of "black history" in mainstream history classes.

More than the doldrums, it is a type of national PTSD. It is not exculpatory or progressive, necessitating criminal justice reform. It is systemic, it is structural, and it is functioning the way it was designed to function, criminalizing by weaponizing "wokeness" with excessive force.

PTSD can be brought on by repeated exposure to racism. For example, the suppression and exclusion of African history has had a fundamentally detrimental effect on both sides of the issue:

White guilt fragility over white privilege is painful.
Black anger/victimization and exclusion is painful.

The pain is exploding onto the streets...
For what is cognitive dissonance if not the absence of direction that religion provides.

Buddhists have koans; Kensho, Satori
Hindus have transcendental meditation. Yoga
Christians have Jesus and the Holy Spirit and Beatitudes.
Native Americans have Great Spirit

Muslims have pillars; Koran

Jews have the Torah

Additionally, Richard M. Bucke (psychiatrist 1901), in Cosmic Consciousness: A Study in the Evolution of the Human Mind, went so far as to say: "The Negro and Australian Aboriginal operate on the animal level of simple consc....impossible to believe that as a race these creatures are self-consc." Nevertheless, Pushkin, Russia's greatest poet, was black, and Dumas, the 3 Musketeers, "All for One and One for All," was black.

In James 1:5-8, which says:

"If any of you lack wisdom, let him ask of God that giveth all men liberally and upbraideth not; and it shall be given him. But let him ask in faith nothing wavering. For he that wavers is like a wave of the sea driven with the wind and tossed. For let not that man think that he shall receive anything of the Lord. A double-minded man is unstable in all His ways."

Balanced by:

For I will restore health to you, and I will heal your wounds, says the Lord, because they have called you an outcast, saying, This is Zion, whom no one seeks after and for whom no one cares! Jeremiah 30:17 AMPC

Do not be conformed to this world (this age), [fashioned after and adapted to its external, superficial customs], but be transformed (changed) by the [entire] renewal of your mind [by its new ideals and its new attitude], so that you may prove [for yourselves] what is the good and acceptable and perfect will of God, even the thing which is good and acceptable and perfect [in His sight for you]. Romans 12:2 AMPC

Chapter 4

One Body In The Beloved

And He made from one [common origin, one source, one blood] all nations of men to settle on the face of the earth, having definitely determined [their] allotted periods of time and the fixed boundaries of their habitation (their settlements, lands, and abodes), So that they should seek God, in the hope that they might feel after Him and find Him, although He is not far from each one of us. Acts 17:26-27 AMPC

Systemic racism. Americans must face it. Healing America's history to include the contributions of African Americans would be a good start. 2 Chronicles 7:14 and Matthew 3:8 would be a good start. See Santa Clara V. Southern Pacific Railroad Co. 118 U.S 394 (1886)

The failure to deconstruct systemic oppression and racism is already spilling out into the streets. Now is the time for change.

An emphasis on 3-ness in the Beloved can bring about a regeneration of one-ness: one body in Christ, the Beloved. The hybrid of science and intelligent design is not enough. A divine reawakening to being one body in Christ is necessary. Not just at funerals. Not just in prisons.

John 17:21 (one); Matthew 7:12 (Golden Rule)

The natural, the supernatural, and the divine must be superseded by the Father, the Son, and the Holy Spirit. Jesus is the true Root. Revelation 22:16! Asking for understanding Psalm 119:130 is healthier than the consequences of settling for the roots of Social Darwinism. For 2 Corinthians 4:3: If our Gospel is vIneiled, it is veiled to those who are perishing. And Hebrews 10:20, Jesus is the Veil.

Jesus is the true Door, John 10:9-11, Revelation 3:8, Matthew 7:14.

It is with unwavering faith that this essay is submitted and will contribute to the effectuation of national healing...

Social Darwinism's survival of the fittest, like veiled Christianity, helped to justify:
Domestic terrorism
Racism
Eugenics
Imperialism
Political conservatism
Social inequality;[1]
And the present criminal justice system is modern-day slavery.

No one after he has lighted a lamp covers it with a vessel or puts it under a [dining table] couch; but he puts it on a lampstand, that those who come in may see the light. For there is nothing hidden that shall not be disclosed, nor anything secret that shall not be known and come out into the open. Luke 8:16-17 AMPC

Nor do men light a lamp and put it under a peck measure, but on a lampstand, and it gives light to all in the house. Matthew 5:15 AMPC

And He said to them, Is the lamp brought in to be put under a peck measure or under a bed, and not [to be put] on the lampstand? Things are hidden temporarily only as a means to revelation.] For there is nothing hidden except to be revealed, nor is anything [temporarily] kept secret except in order that it may be made known. Mark 4:21-22 AMPC

Which is His body, the fullness of Him who fills and completes all things in all [believers]. Ephesians 1:23 AMP

Christ fills all things everywhere with Himself.

[1]Informational topics on Social Darwinism obtained from Google search

Chapter 5

Blacks As Vacuous

The depiction of blacks as *vacuous*: blank, mindless, and *wanting to be noticed* is as counterintuitive and dangerous as a war on intelligence - a.k.a. a war on woke.

> *God is [already] beginning to arise, and His enemies to scatter; let them also who hate Him flee before Him!...The Lord gives the word [of power]; the women who bear and publish [the news] are a great host. The kings of the enemies' armies, they flee, they flee! She who tarries at home divides the spoil [left behind]. Psalms 68:1; 11-12 AMPC*

The reframing and relabeling of comprehensive black history as a precursor to overt dehumanization and objectification (Lynch mob mentality) is as dangerous as the Lynch mob itself. Contemporary techniques of flooding the internet media with Willie Lynch letters in innumerable numbers are a virtual frenzied celebration of torment which, absent comprehensive black history, is equivalent to being immoral.

The teachings that slavery brought with it a personal benefit to slaves, as currently being required, are as immoral as the institution of slavery itself and are without socially redemptive value. It is lying, on steroids, and is nothing short of mendacious propaganda... Prager University is a prime example! It is propaganda such as that which, in the case of Carrie Buck, inspired Hitler; and, in the case of Richard M. Bucke, inspired him to say that insane whites are superior to blacks because of blacks being vacuous or mindless. Since 1901, the dangers have been self-evident.

Chapter 6

Vacuous vs. Double Consciousness

An appreciation and acknowledgment of double consciousness prepares the mind for an understanding of the difference between Spiritual insights versus bigotry and dominance games. For example, the acceptance of the existence of multiple, actually innumerable, versions of Willie Lynch letters on the *internet as required* reading is bigotry, and it contradicts the very premise of hypervigilance on the part of black people in America concerning the subject of black history.

Increasingly, this history is being outright banned by being labeled wokeism, critical race theory (CRT), cancel culture, and D.E.I. The very existence of comprehensive black history, culture, and religious perspectives has no place of mainstream acknowledgment because of this, except to be hijacked, misquoted, and placed out of context.

Take, for example, such statements as Martin Luther King's "content of character". Used out of context against blacks it is as much a paradigm shift as Carl Van Vecheten's book relabeling the Harlem Renaissance. Being innocuous, non-threatening, and harmless is no buffer to being relegated to obscurity. Youth inaugural poet Laureate Amanda Gorman's work has been banned! Additionally, Dr. Chester M. Pierce, a black Harvard University tenured professor of education and psychiatry, is relegated to obscurity in spite of the fact that he created the term "microaggression" and was a senior creative consultant for Sesame Street.

And again, ironically, microaggression means indirect, subtle, or unintentional discrimination against members of a marginalized group.

The definition of "woke" changes depending on who you ask. But *tuning out* remains the same and results in devastating confusion. Such a loaded and veiled term as "woke" is worthy of a clear, unambiguous, and concise definition, and yet Webster, Collins, Cambridge and Oxford dictionary definitions are offered online, resulting in a literal quagmire and plethora of explanations. The definition is thereby *veiled*.

The 21st-century Republican right protests the teaching of comprehensive history because it makes him "uncomfortable." When comprehensive history teaches, in the words of Frederick Douglass, "The white man's happiness cannot be purchased by the black man's misery." The foregoing equals an insidious symbiotic relationship if and when the black person does or does not correct it with so-called hypervigilance. And the white person tunes out the information! The definition is thereby *veiled*.

Chapter 7
Wanting To Be Noticed

Wanting to be noticed reeks of white privilege when applied to blacks who are asserting themselves or the rights of others.

The phraseology is a miasma of condescension, an insult to intelligence, and a dazzling flash of the suppression of the truth as well as an expression of believed superiority - an excuse to tune out.

Chapter 8

History Written By Victors

The phrase, "history is written by the victors" looms in its assertion of victory. However, it may be countered by James Baldwin, who said, "People who imagine that history flatters them are impaled on their history like a butterfly on a pin and become incapable of seeing or changing themselves or the world. This is a place in which it seems to me most white Americans find themselves. Impaled... They are *Dimly* or *Vividly* aware that the history they have fed themselves is a lie. But they do not know how to *release* themselves from it, and they suffer enormously from the resulting personal incoherence." Instead of personal growth.

As stated before, this is devastating confusion due to tuning out. Additionally, however, James Baldwin's *complicated* views on religion distinguish his work categorically. This is undeniably a tricky landscape.

Nevertheless, it was Frederick Douglass who said, "No man can put a chain about the ankle of his fellow man without at last finding the other end fastened about his own neck."

Chapter 9

Thoughtlessness

Finally, "I have found that to make a contented slave it's necessary to make a thoughtless one" from Narrative of the Life of Frederick Douglass. So, you see, tuning out appears to be the next best thing to the actual making of a vacuous, thoughtless one. But which one?

In fact, some libraries in Houston, Texas, are being converted from libraries to disciplinary centers under the New Education System (NES) in 2023. It is not expected that we can see the parallels between Willie Lynch's making of a slave and Frederick Douglass's making of a thoughtless one. This is not veiled language!

Chapter 10

Aesop Tuned Out

Why, the writer of fables who is universally taught to babies in the crib and five year old's in school with some of the first moral and common sense lessons of life is Aesop: Tortoise and Hare, The Boy Who Cried Wolf, North Wind and the Sun and many, many others. 620-574 B.C., Aesop was black. This black history has been kept in obscurity in America. Is it hyper-vigilant to point this out? Perhaps. Yes. It is actually a social responsibility to be assertive about it and proactive in the face of being tuned out. *Countless* others are tuned out every day in everyday inventions and accomplishments.

A reasonable person, *white or black*, distinguishes between comprehensive black history and so-called classical history as easily as he distinguishes the rabbit and the duck in Kuhn's famous illusion. They are seen as simply a matter of perspective. On the other hand, a biased person attaches value to one perspective rather than another. The value assignment can also be seen in the glass half-empty or half-full illustration. But the difference is the half-full perspective is favored or valued over the half-empty perspective. The bias is often subtly turned to bigotry where race is concerned. And reasonableness is subjective!

Chapter 11

Woke

So, too, is "woke/woke mob" subjective. In black vernacular, it means awake, aware, and alert to racial prejudice and discrimination. In white vernacular, it gets so complicated as to be veiled because it is pejorative and used to criticize people for seeing injustice where it does not exist! It also pertains to affirmative action, national anthem kneeling, named sports teams, statues, flags, and reparations! All symbols of unreconciled contradictions in America.

As for those who would detract from what is being said here: Psalm 68:11-12 and Psalm 68:1 AMPC.

Chapter 12

Scripture

God saw the Israelites and took knowledge of them and concerned Himself about them [knowing all, understanding, remembering all]. Exodus 2:25 AMPC

O Lord, you have searched me [thoroughly] and have known me. You know my downsitting and my uprising; You understand my thought afar off. You sift and search out my path and my lying down, and You are acquainted with all my ways. For there is not a word in my tongue [still unuttered], but, behold, O Lord, You know it altogether. Psalm 139:1-4 AMPC

If My people, who are called by My name, shall humble themselves, pray, seek, crave, and require of necessity My face and turn from their wicked ways, then will I hear from heaven, forgive their sin, and heal their land. 2 Chronicles 7:14 KJV

Who made heaven and earth, the sea, and all that is in them, Who keeps truth and is faithful forever Psalm 146:6 AMPC

Who can discern his lapses and errors? Clear me from hidden [and unconscious] faults. Keep back Your servant also from presumptuous sins; let them not have dominion over me! Then shall I be blameless, and I shall be innocent and clear of great transgression. Let the words of my mouth and the meditation of my heart be acceptable in Your sight, O Lord, my [firm, impenetrable] Rock and my Redeemer. Psalm 19:12-14 AMPC

Chapter 13

Return or No Return
to Heaven

Hebrews 11:16-16 AMPC

Centuries of Veiled Christianity account for not only un-reconciled contradictions but also the popular and outright rejection of Christianity in favor of Nihilism or the rejection of all religious and moral principles in the belief that life itself is meaningless. Domestic Terrorism has often been the result! While on the other hand, many atrocities have been committed in the very name of God...

As we have now somewhat examined the scourge of racism with its stereotype of black people, may this be the time that the stronghold elements of racism are eradicated for *ALL PEOPLE.*

Chapter 14

Scriptural Conclusion

May dignity be restored to the afflicted according to Acts 5:41-42, wherein the afflicted and persecuted are "dignified by the indignity" and, according to Isaiah 61:11 AMPC, the self-fulfilling power of His Word.

Study and be eager and do your utmost to present your-self to God approved (tested by trial), a workman who has no cause to be ashamed, correctly analyzing and ac-curately dividing [rightly handling and skillfully teaching] the Word of Truth. 2 Timothy 2:15 AMPC

For we are not wrestling with flesh and blood [contend-ing only with physical opponents], but against the despot-isms, against the powers, against [the master spirits who are] the world rulers of this present darkness, against the spirit forces of wickedness in the heavenly (supernatural) sphere. Ephesians 6:12 AMPC

For the weapons of our warfare are not physical [weap-ons of flesh and blood], but they are mighty before God for the overthrow and destruction of strongholds... 2 Corinthi-ans 10:4. AMPC

Roll your works upon the Lord [commit and trust them wholly to Him; He will cause your thoughts to become agreeable to His will, and] so shall your plans be estab-lished and succeed. Proverbs 16:3 AMPC

Chapter 15

Mansions

Now those people who talk as they did show plainly that they are in search of a fatherland (their own country). If they had been thinking with [HOMESICK] REMEMBRANCE of that country from which they were emigrants, they would have found constant opportunity to return to it. But the truth is that they were yearning for and aspiring to a better and more desirable country, that is, a heavenly [one]. For that reason God is not ashamed to be called their God [even to be surnamed their God—the God of Abraham, Isaac, and Jacob], for He has prepared a city for them. Hebrews 11:14-16 AMPC

Do not let your hearts be troubled (distressed, agitated). You believe in and adhere to and trust in and rely on God; believe in and adhere to and trust in and rely also on Me. In My Father's house there are many dwelling places (homes). If it were not so, I would have told you; for I am going away to prepare a place for you. And when (if) I go and make ready a place for you, I will come back again and will take you to Myself, that where I am you may be also. And [to the place] where I am going, you know the way. Thomas said to

Him, Lord, we do not know where You are going, so how can we know the way? Jesus said to him, I am the Way and the Truth and the Life; no one comes to the Father except by (through) Me. John 14:1-6 AMPC

Nor will people say, Look! Here [it is]! or, See, [it is] there! For behold, the kingdom of God is within you [in your hearts] and among you [surrounding you]. Luke 17:21AMPC

From that time Jesus began to preach, crying out, Repent change your mind for the better, heartily amend your ways, with abhorrence of your past sins), for the kingdom of heaven is at hand. Matthew 4:17 AMPC

MANSIONS ARE STATES OF CONSCIOUSNESS, AND METANOIA IS ORIGINAL GREEK WORD FOR REPENT...

Acknowledgements

Pastor Willie Graham and Co-Pastor Barbara Graham: Love, personal growth, and providence grace your ministry. Thank you so very much!

Adrienne Stewart Psalm 91; John 14:1-6
Vincit Omnia Veritas

Ann: Thank you so very much

Arthur (Big Boy) Crudup: You are not forgotten

Banks Family Descendants: You are nestled in my heart

Byron L. Crudup: An absolute praiseworthy genius; well done

Camille Cotton: Psalm 91; John 14:1-6
Vincit Omnia Veritas

Dominique: Thank you so very much

Gloria Johnson: Psalm 34:8

Isaiah: You encouraged this project in its infancy

Justin Jones: Psalm 143:5 Ephesians 1:17-19

Justin Pearson: Psalm 143:5 Ephesians 1:17-19

Dr. Michelle Carter and Edward Carter: Your selfless influence has deeply inspired this project from its infancy

Sis Nakisha Pendleton: Blessings and gratitude for your skill transcribing my handwriting, your patience and encouragement in this project

Nikisha Sims: Founder of Warrior Princess Nation Publishing. Overwhelming gratitude

Paula LeDoux: Thank you so very much

Raquel Crudup: Sis, your staunch support is greatly appreciated

Ron: Our daughters are amazing!

Stephen: Your work is still going forward

UC Berkeley Ethnic Studies Department: You were there when I needed you

CBLF Ministries: Church Family! Thank you one and all! 1 Thessalonians 5:11; Hebrews 6:10; John 13:35

Missionary Vivian Crear: Your assistance helped me manifest this book

Imara, Theresa, and Leslie: Cultural revelations of courage and resilience belong to you

Rev. Annette (Banks) Johnson: Special Thanks!

About The Author

Barbara was born in Oakland, CA, the second child of Seabie L. Crudup and Odessa B. Crudup. Extremely contemplative, she was educated in the home and at Oakland Technical High School. She then studied for three years at UC Berkeley as a social science field major at the burgeoning and renowned Ethnic Studies Department.

After the birth of her beloved daughters Camille and Adrienne and meeting life's challenges in the corporate world, she graduated from New College of California School of Law San Francisco with a Juris Doctor Degree. She qualified to travel to Athens, Greece, to study mediation with a select group of law students, where she gained an important perspective on the U.S.A.'s racial dilemma.

After speaking before the Body of Christ at church one day, she was observed to be gifted by the Holy Spirit in the world of words, their meaning, and interpretation. The Veiled Definition and The Door Of No Return is a product of that gift.

She joined Christian Body Life Fellowship (CBLF), pastored by Dr. Willie Graham and Dr. Barbara Graham in 2013. Over the years, she has participated in teaching Sunday school, special speaking events, and being president of the Mother's Board. She has also participated in a group of women from all over the Bay Area called Women of Wisdom.

Barbara has been privileged to mentor and advise younger women according to Titus 2:4-8, NLT

Barbara loves the Lord Jesus Christ, gives Him preeminence in her life, surrenders to His authority, and surrenders her work to His authority according to His will.